Inventions That CHANGED the WORLD

How Twitter Changed the World

Kaitlyn Duling

New York

Published in 2019 by Cavendish Square Publishing, LLC
243 5th Avenue, Suite 136, New York, NY 10016

Copyright © 2019 by Cavendish Square Publishing, LLC

First Edition

No part of this publication may be reproduced, stored in a retrieval system, or transmitted in any form or by any means—electronic, mechanical, photocopying, recording, or otherwise—without the prior permission of the copyright owner. Request for permission should be addressed to Permissions, Cavendish Square Publishing, 243 5th Avenue, Suite 136, New York, NY 10016. Tel (877) 980-4450; fax (877) 980-4454.

Website: cavendishsq.com

This publication represents the opinions and views of the author based on his or her personal experience, knowledge, and research. The information in this book serves as a general guide only. The author and publisher have used their best efforts in preparing this book and disclaim liability rising directly or indirectly from the use and application of this book.

All websites were available and accurate when this book was sent to press.

Library of Congress Cataloging-in-Publication Data

Names: Duling, Kaitlyn, author.
Title: How twitter changed the world / Kaitlyn Duling.
Description: First edition. | New York : Cavendish Square, 2019. | Series: Inventions that changed the world | Audience: Grades 5 to 8. | Includes bibliographical references and index.
Identifiers: LCCN 2018024818 (print) | LCCN 2018026000 (ebook) | ISBN 9781502641212 (ebook) | ISBN 9781502641205 (library bound) | ISBN 9781502641199 (pbk.)
Subjects: LCSH: Twitter--Juvenile literature. | Online social networks--Social aspects--Juvenile literature.
Classification: LCC HM743.T95 (ebook) | LCC HM743.T95 D85 2019 (print) | DDC 302.30285--dc23
LC record available at https://lccn.loc.gov/2018024818

Editorial Director: David McNamara
Editor: Kristen Susienka
Copy Editor: Alex Tessman
Associate Art Director: Alan Sliwinski
Designer: Joe Parenteau
Production Coordinator: Karol Szymczuk
Photo Research: J8 Media

The photographs in this book are used by permission and through the courtesy of: Cover, p. 1 Shay Bakstad/Shutterstock.com; p. 4 CJG – Technology/Alamy Stock Photo; p. 6 0meer/Shutterstock.com; p. 7 hocus-focus/iStock; p. 8 James D. Morgan/Getty Images; p. 11 John Gomez/Shutterstock.com; p. 12 David Paul Morris/Bloomberg/Getty Images; p. 15 Jack Dorsey/Flickr.com/182613360/CC BY-SA 2.0; p. 17 GCShutter/Shutterstock.com; p. 19 Jack Dorsey/Newspix/Getty Images; p. 25 Bethany Clarke/Getty Images; p. 26 Lars niki/Corbis/Getty Images; p. 27 Kyodo News/Getty Images; p. 28 Eva-Katalin/iStock; p. 31 Hero Images/Getty Images; p. 34 Gorodenkoff/Shutterstock.com; p. 36 Vincent Brown/Flickr.com/36903961456/CC BY-SA 2.0; p. 39 solomon7/Shutterstock.com; p. 41 Sean Gallup/Getty Images; p. 43 Brent Payne/Flickr.com/4685873543/CC BY-SA 2.0; p. 44 David McNew/Getty Images; p. 47 Chris Ratcliffe/Bloomberg/Getty Images; p. 48 Ibrahim.ID/Wikimedia Commons/File:Socialmedia-pm.png/CC BY-SA 4.0; p. 49 Omer Messinger/NurPhoto/Getty Images; p. 53 simonkr/iStock; p. 54 Natee Meepian/Shutterstock.com.

Printed in the United States of America

CONTENTS

ONE The Twitter Difference 5

TWO Bird Beginnings 13

THREE Twitter Takes Over 29

FOUR Leaving a Legacy 45

Glossary 56

Further Information 58

Selected Bibliography 60

Index 62

About the Author 64

Today, users can access Twitter via their laptop, smartphone, tablet, or another mobile device.

CHAPTER ONE

The Twitter Difference

Do you remember where you were on the night your favorite team won the big game? Do you recall how you learned about the outcome of the last presidential election? What about the last time a famous celebrity died—how did you know? You may have heard the news from a friend or family member via text, or even in person. But chances are, you have found out about a number of important events while scrolling through social media. The term "social media" includes all of the apps and websites we use in order to communicate with others. Facebook, Instagram, Snapchat, and Twitter are all types of social media. We use them to look at pictures, send messages, and share our thoughts.

These days, our worlds seem to revolve around social media. People upload images of their most important life

Television is still a popular source of news, but many people are turning to apps like Twitter in order to get the most up-to-date news and opinions.

events, like weddings, birthdays, and graduations. They share the most boring details too. Did you ever wonder what your aunt had for dinner last night? You might find out if you visit her Facebook page. Social media brings us happy news—engagements and new jobs! And it brings bad news—arguments, debates, bullying, violence, and more. Sometimes it seems like these sites and apps are bursting with pictures, videos, words, and information. It can be overwhelming. There is one application, however, that has based itself on *limiting* the amount that can be shared. In fact, this app restricts your message to 280 characters! Out of all the applications (or apps), sites, and options out there, Twitter is unique.

A Different Kind of App

While Facebook, Snapchat, and other apps are designed to help us socialize with friends, Twitter is expansive. Over the years, it has grown away from its humble beginnings as a platform for sharing short, 140-character messages, its original character limit. Today, Twitter is a place where major news breaks and serious discussions are had—between millions of strangers.

In fact, each month, Twitter is growing. By last official count, the application had over 330 million active users each month! This makes it one of the most popular social networks in the world, even though Facebook, WeChat, and other brands are popular as well. On Twitter, people can connect with friends, family, classmates, and coworkers. But they can also connect with celebrities, politicians, athletes, and even brands. The most-followed Twitter accounts are those of Katy Perry, Justin Bieber, Barack Obama, and Rihanna. With hundreds of millions of followers each, these celebrities are able to reach a huge portion of the public, often with just a few words or sentences.

There are so many applications to choose from. Twitter is just one of many social media apps available to smartphone users.

The Twitter Difference 7

President Obama was hugely popular on Twitter when he was in office, and he continues to be a fan favorite. Here he gives a talk in Sydney, Australia, in 2018.

    Twitter not only has breadth, but it has depth. This is another characteristic that makes it unique. In August 2017, two-thirds of Americans reported that they got some of their news on Twitter. That isn't a portion of Twitter users—it's over half of the people living in the United States! Over the years, this number has continued its steady growth. Sometimes Twitter has the news before other, more "traditional" sources, like newspapers and television stations.

TWEETING WITHOUT TWITTER

You can tweet through the Twitter application or website. You can also tweet through clients. Clients are owned by other companies. They might look a little unique and work differently, but they also allow you to tweet. Over the years, client apps have included Tweetbot, Tweetdeck, Twitteriffic, Tweetie, Hootsuite, Buffer, Chirp, Tweeten, and more.

Why would someone use a client instead of the regular Twitter app? Some of these clients make it easier to use more than one Twitter account at once. Others allowed you to Tweet from specific platforms, like iPhones, Androids, and Mac computers, before Twitter was available. Clients can make it possible to schedule tweets, make lists, and access other features. Clients occasionally run faster or appear to be less "buggy" than the original. Companies make these clients with the hope that users will like using their app better than the Twitter app. Sometimes, they succeed!

On a January day in 2009, an airplane crashed into the Hudson River in New York City. CNN wasn't the first to report it. The radio wasn't either. The news was broken by a photo posted on Twitter! This is just one example of the ways in which Twitter has become much more than a social media platform. Some of the most liked and "retweeted," or shared, thoughts on Twitter have come from politicians. News, such as updates on weather disasters, up-to-the-minute accounts of violent incidents, and notifications of celebrity deaths have made Twitter the place to go for immediate news. Before television journalists can provide commentary, Twitter users are already talking. Analysis shows that about 87 percent of the world's leaders are on Twitter. For those who want to interact with influential people from all across the globe, the world really is at our fingertips.

Through words, pictures, and even short videos, users can share almost anything on Twitter. People flock to the application for news, opinions, sports, election results, jokes, personal stories, and so much more. Twitter is

DID YOU KNOW:

Have you ever seen the little blue checkmark next to someone's Twitter handle? This means it is a verified account. Celebrities, politicians, athletes, and other popular people can have their accounts verified. This helps Twitter users know that the account is really that person.

Twitter helps people stand up for what they believe is right. It has created a platform for activists to organize rallies like this one, part of the #BlackLivesMatter movement.

a platform for personal voice, as well as the voices of groups. Many groups that have been traditionally left out of larger conversations, such as women, LGBTQ people, and people of color, have taken to Twitter as a tool to help them speak out. On Twitter, celebrities and politicians have voices, but everyday people do too. There are no gatekeepers—anyone can join Twitter. Of course, the platform has its share of abuse, bullying, lying, and other issues. Many communication tools have these problems. In the long line of history, however, Twitter has found its place within a very specific cultural moment. It continues to gain users, break news stories, and, ultimately, encourage conversation. Going forward, it will be these conversations that decide whether Twitter will remain relevant or fade behind other upcoming social media and communication platforms.

Biz Stone, seated on the right, talks about Twitter during the 2014 SXSW festival.

Bird Beginnings

The story of how Twitter went from a humble side project to a huge communication tool is a fascinating one. Like many other early social media platforms, Twitter began as a passion project shared by a group of friends. It wasn't dreamed up by a company's research department. Its success was not guaranteed or even planned. Though the company is now worth billions of dollars, its founders could only dream about that amount of money at first. The group of young men who founded Twitter got their start while working on another project, Odeo.

Odeo

Founded in 2005, Odeo was a website that served as a podcast directory. Users could search for podcasts, explore lists of podcasts, and discover new content. A podcast is an audio file, usually available for streaming or download online. Podcasts are often formatted as series. They might have interviews, stories, skits, news, or other verbal content. In 2005, podcasting was just becoming popular. This was around the time that iPods and other digital mp3 players were taking off. Through Odeo, podcast fans could share their favorite podcasts with their friends and publish to various social networks. As it was getting started, Odeo had a small following, but it wasn't a very popular site. The official founders, Evan Williams and Biz Stone, weren't sure what move to make next. After Apple launched iTunes, their site started to become irrelevant. People could explore podcasts faster and easier through iTunes.

One of the other early employees at Odeo was a man named Jack Dorsey. Dorsey was a student at New York University, and his brain was full of creative ideas. As the story goes, Dorsey suggested to Williams and Stone a new project he was dreaming up. It was a messaging service that allowed small groups of friends to share status updates, almost like group texting. Dorsey was in love with the idea of one's personal "status" and how that could be shared. The three friends had a brainstorming session about the idea, deciding to call it "Twttr." Legend has it that an Odeo employee named Noah Glass came up with the name Twttr originally. Unfortunately, his name has largely been left out of the company's story.

Popular myths about the company say that the friends were inspired by Flickr, a photo-sharing website. They had also tossed around the names "Dodgeball" and

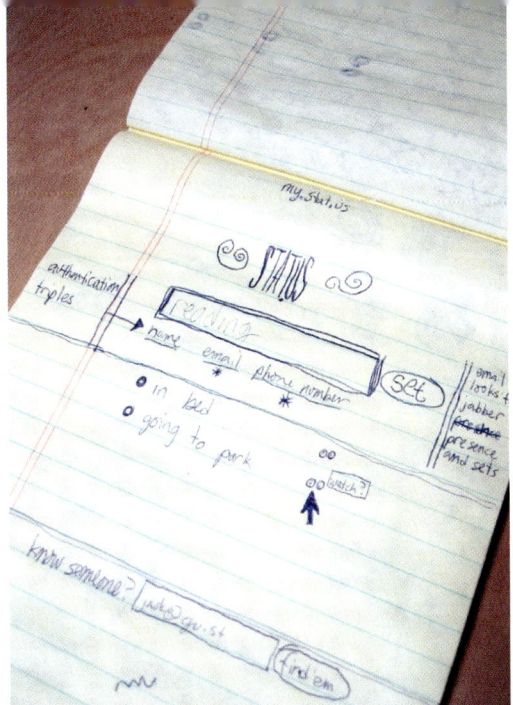

This image shows some of Jack Dorsey's original drawings. Sketches like this one helped him to dream up the Twitter application.

"Friendstalker," but Twttr was the one that stuck. It didn't hurt that taking vowels out of the name made it more likely that the site could get a website name, since it had a unique look.

In February 2006, the Twttr idea was shared with the rest of the Odeo company. At the time, there were about fourteen employees, and they all heard the same pitch: A system that allowed a person to text one number, which would send a mass message out to friends. Around the same time, Noah Glass and the others decided to change the official name of the product to "Twitter." Though Evan Williams remained skeptical, the new product was finally taking shape. It began to gain popularity with people around the Odeo office. News was shared. Conversations were had. And Odeo employees began to rack up large cell phone bills due to all of their Twitter usage. The group knew it had something good.

Who Owns Twitter?

This is where the story gets a little confusing. After iTunes was released, Odeo began to fail financially. In the fall of 2006, some of the founders decided to use their own money to purchase the company from its investors. This is called a "buyback." Evan Williams, Jack Dorsey, Biz Stone, and other employees bought the company. In doing so, they also purchased the rights to Twitter. Williams, Odeo's CEO, wrote the following in his letter to investors:

> By the way, Twitter (http://twitter.com), which you may have read about, is one of the pieces of value that I see in Odeo, but it's much too early to tell what's there. Almost two months after launch, Twitter has less than 5,000 registered users.

It's hard to say whether Dorsey, Williams, or the other employees knew about Twitter's potential. Now it was in the hands of the few who had bought back the company. Some, like Williams and Dorsey, were solidly in that group. Others, like Noah Glass, who had come up with the original name, were no longer involved.

Just a few months earlier, Jack Dorsey had sent the very first tweet. It read, "just setting up my twttr." The tweet was sent on March 21, 2006, right before 10:00 p.m. After that, the Twittersphere was never quiet again. Employee Dom Sagolla said it best in the thirty-eighth tweet ever sent: "Oh, this is going to be addictive."

It still took a few months, however, for Twitter to truly take off. Its biggest launch happened at the spring

These days, few people leave home without a smartphone. We use them to talk, text, post to social media apps, check the time ... and so much more!

of 2007 South by Southwest Interactive conference, also known as SXSW. The event brings together all sorts of businesses, creative people, and media. It was the perfect place for Twitter. It is held each year in Austin, Texas. In 2007, Twitter paid $11,000 to put a version of the Twitter service up on flat-paneled screens in the hallways. At SXSW, attendees could sign up automatically by texting a number.

The marketing plan was a hit. Before SXSW, the site published about twenty thousand messages per day. After? It broke sixty thousand per day and added numerous dedicated users. One *Gawker* writer, reporting on the conference, said, "In the next year, Twitter could make a Facebook-sized blowup among the general public." His guess would end up being eerily accurate.

The Main Players

Some inventions are dreamed up by individuals. Maria Beasley is credited with inventing the life raft.

Alexander Graham Bell made the first telephone. But some innovations, like Twitter, need a group of strong minds. Working together, four men brought Twitter out of their notepads and into existence.

Jack Dorsey

Jack Dorsey wasn't born into the world of tech startups. In fact, he grew up deep in the Midwest, far away from the technological center of Silicon Valley in California. He was born on November 19, 1976, in St. Louis, Missouri. From a young age, Dorsey had a keen interest in computers. He began playing with programming in high school, focusing on software that helped taxi and delivery companies dispatch their vehicles and bicycles. He built the software on a Macintosh computer that his dad purchased for him. This was his first introduction to real-time internet services. Little did Dorsey know that he would go on to create a service known for its up-to-the-moment news and communication abilities.

Dorsey followed his passion for tech into the Missouri University of Science and Technology. After a brief stint there, he transferred to New York University, finally traveling to the coast, far from his home. While Dorsey was a passionate learner, he dropped out of college before receiving his degree. This isn't uncommon for founders of tech startups. Bill Gates (Microsoft), Steve Jobs (Apple), and Mark Zuckerberg (Facebook) all ended their quests for degrees. After dropping out, each of them went on to create some of the most successful companies of the twenty-first century. Dorsey did the same. He moved to

Twitter CEO Jack Dorsey signed up for the popular blogging site LiveJournal in 2000. It inspired him to start working on Twitter.

Oakland, California. In 2000, he formed a company to support his dispatch software.

That very year, Dorsey sketched out the earliest ideas for Twitter on a yellow legal pad. He was inspired by LiveJournal and hoped to create something that was even more immediate than the blogging platform. The idea stayed on the paper and in his head though, as he devoted most of his time to the dispatch company. Unfortunately, the company fired him in 2002, and Dorsey quickly moved back to Missouri, where he stayed until 2005. In the years when he wasn't working in tech, Dorsey had all sorts of side jobs. He even worked as a masseuse for a time! By 2005, he could no longer ignore his itch to get back into the programming world, and made the move to California. To support his rent in California, he found a coding job on Craigslist. In his spare time, Dorsey hung out at coffee shops. One was Caffe Centro in San Francisco. It was there that Dorsey bumped into Evan Williams. Williams was already established in the tech and business worlds.

Bird Beginnings

JACK DORSEY: TWITTER CEO

Not only did Jack Dorsey create Twitter, but he is also the company's chief executive officer, or CEO. This is the highest-ranking position in most companies. As CEO, Dorsey makes decisions, manages operations, and more. Dorsey rejoined Twitter in this position in 2015. Now, he is CEO for both Twitter and Square, a credit-card-payment company. The two headquarters are actually across the street from each other, so he doesn't have to travel far to switch between jobs. Usually, Dorsey spends the morning at the Twitter office and moves over to Square in the afternoon.

For the last three years, Dorsey has refused a salary from Twitter. This sends a powerful message about his belief in the company. Of course, Dorsey still gets "paid." He owns about eighteen million shares in Twitter, which are worth hundreds of millions of dollars. He also owns shares in Square that are worth over $3 billion.

He agreed to hire Dorsey as a coder at Odeo. It was the environment at Odeo, far from his Midwestern roots, that gave Dorsey the time, space, and resources to finally work on Twitter, taking it from scratch pad to real-life product.

Evan Williams

Much like his eventual cofounder Jack Dorsey, Evan Williams was born in the Midwest. He grew up in Clarks, Nebraska, where he was born on March 23, 1972. In another striking similarity to Dorsey, Williams attended the University of Nebraska for a short time before dropping out to pursue his career dreams in information science. He secured freelance and part-time positions at companies like Hewlett-Packard and Intel before cofounding a range of businesses: Pyra Labs, Blogger, and Odeo. Blogger was by far the most successful, as it was one of the very first applications to make blogging an easy and user-friendly task. Blogging refers to the writing and sharing of short, nonfiction, often personal stories online. Unlike Facebook or other social media platforms, blogs are usually meant to be shared with the general public.

As Blogger became successful, Williams was named one of *MIT Technology Review* magazine's "top 100 innovators under age 35" list, as well as "Person of the Year" by *PC Magazine*. All of that success added up, and on February 17, 2003, Google announced its purchase of Pyra Labs and Blogger. At the time, Blogger hosted over one million blogs, about two hundred thousand of which were active. The sale was viewed as a sign that blogging had really taken off. At the time, Williams had just six employees at the company. He had been running it out of his own home. His business had only recently started to make money when Williams added a premium version of Blogger to the site, which users could access for a fee. After the sale of Pyra and Blogger, Williams was finally free to found Odeo, the company that would launch Twitter in the coming years.

Biz Stone

Another key player in the Twitter story is Biz Stone, one of the original founders from Odeo. Christopher "Biz" Stone was born on March 10, 1974, and grew up in Wellesley, Massachusetts. Just like his Odeo/Twitter colleagues, Stone attended college at both Northeastern University and University of Massachusetts–Boston, before dropping out to pursue a career. Though this was a risky move, Stone found early success. In 1999, he signed on as the creative director of Xanga, a blogging platform. He also started a blogging company called Genius Labs. While not as popular as Blogger, Genius Labs was acquired by Google in 2003. Around the same time that both of their blogging sites were purchased by Google, Stone and Williams began to exchange emails. Eventually, Stone moved to Silicon Valley.

"Silicon Valley" refers to a specific area in northern California, in the south San Francisco Bay Area. Over the years, it has become a popular place for tech companies, innovation, and social media. At one time, there were a high number of silicon chip makers in the area. Today, it is filled with big businesses and start-up companies,

> **DID YOU KNOW:**
>
> As a company, Twitter has purchased other businesses. In 2012, it bought Vine, a video app that quickly closed. In 2015, it bought Periscope, a live-streaming service. Over time, Twitter has acquired over fifty different companies.

but the name stuck. It was in Silicon Valley that Stone joined the Blogger team at Google, eventually leaving to be an integral part of Odeo.

Noah Glass

The fourth and final piece of the Twitter quad is Noah Glass. In 2011, Glass went public with complaints about being left out of popular stories about Twitter's origins. When people reference Twitter's founding, they often cite Evan Williams and Jack Dorsey, but don't always mention Glass. However, as a member of Odeo, Glass was instrumental in the founding of Twitter. In fact, he is credited as the person who came up with the app's name. Before Odeo, Glass dropped out of college to work at Industrial Light and Magic. This is an industrial effects company founded by George Lucas, the creator of the *Star Wars* movies. He stayed active in the internet tech world, working on various projects until joining Odeo.

After Jack Dorsey came up with the idea for Twitter and began to explore it at Odeo, Glass got on board with the new app. He helped to pitch the board of executives.

He came up with the original name "Twttr" and helped change it to its now-famous name, Twitter. Some of the earliest versions of the company even existed completely on Glass's own laptop. In July 2006, just as Twitter was becoming a trend, Glass was asked to leave the company. Amidst a failing marriage and the stress of life at a start-up company, his coworkers thought his personality had become unpredictable.

Growth and Evolution

After its flashy premier at the SXSW festival in 2007, Twitter began to grow. Since then, it hasn't stopped. Many start-ups and web companies fail in a few years as popularity wears off. Twitter, though, has remained popular. In 2007, the site posted about four hundred thousand tweets every four months. A year later, over one hundred million tweets were posted in that same time. This was a huge jump! Suddenly, users began to connect with friends, family, celebrities, and more. Everyone had something to say, and they wanted to say it on Twitter. Unfortunately, with all of that discussion, there was no simple way to explore the Twitterverse easily. Then, the hashtag was born.

Today, across social media platforms, hashtags (#) are used to link popular subjects. A hashtag is included before a word or phrase. When they click on, search for, or follow that hashtag, readers can see the posts of people who are discussing a certain theme. Hashtags are used for big and small events. They are used for sports, weddings, birthdays, awards shows, and more. They have been used by social movements and politicians. A hashtag can bring people together in conversation. How in the world did this start?

According to Chris Messina, a former Google employee, the hashtag began during the 2007 SXSW. Twitter users in California were annoyed by all of the posts about the festival. They felt that the updates were irrelevant to their own lives, and didn't want to read about it. An active user, Messina proposed that Twitter adopt "channels" for different subjects. But he didn't just send an email—he went to the Twitter offices, walked up to Biz Stone, and made his suggestion of using the "pound" symbol to tag posts. Stone thought the idea was interesting and told Messina to try it out. He did, and a few months later—hashtags were everywhere. They weren't fully embraced by the app until 2009, when they became searchable. After that, the hashtag moved to other platforms. Instagram adopted them in 2010. Users started using them on Facebook. Today, "hashtag" is a common term that people use in day-to-day language, internet use, and even on T-shirts and in jokes.

Though it was "born" on Twitter, the hashtag was an answer to one of Twitter's original flaws. Unorganized

Some hashtags are single words, while others are entire phrases. This is what a hashtag looks like on Twitter.

content was a major problem and complaint from users. By using the hashtag, Messina created an entirely new way of organizing information in the digital age.

Hashtags were a necessary component. It's possible that the app wouldn't have seen such extreme growth without them. By some counts, there are over two billion search queries through Twitter per day, and users tweet about five hundred million times a day, often more. About 42 percent of users open the app each day. Without hashtags, those five hundred million tweets would be a lot of noise.

Throughout its short history, Twitter has had its share of ups and downs. Whenever it rolls out a new version or update, critics complain. Changes are supposed to help the app perform better, but many users don't appreciate it when their favorite website suddenly looks different. The company needs to listen to users because all of that use is how it attracts investors and marketers and continues to make money.

It may sound crazy, but Twitter didn't make a profit until 2018! Before that, it paid for itself through advertising and investments. In 2013, Twitter announced that it would file an Initial Public Offering, or IPO. With an IPO, people can buy shares of a company on the stock market. This

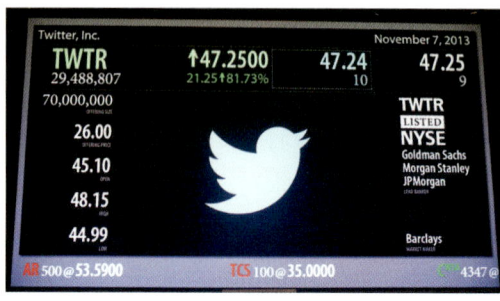

Twitter is listed on the New York Stock Exchange. A screen like this one tells people how much money a share of the company is worth at any given time.

26   How Twitter Changed the World

Twitter is headquartered in San Francisco, California. Many technology companies are based in San Francisco and other cities around the state.

helps raise money to keep the company going, and those who own stock hope to earn money as the stock goes up in value. Facebook filed its own IPO in 2012.

Moving Forward

The four founding "fathers" of Twitter certainly didn't know that they had such a potentially impactful and profitable company on their hands when they sent the first few tweets from within the Odeo office. They may not have known it in the coming years either, when the platform started to become popular. Twitter had its fair share of critics—those who felt that the idea was just another way for people to share irrelevant information, some who didn't like the look, or interface, of the platform, and plenty of social networks that believed they could make a better product. But Twitter has survived through its first decade. Today, it is flying into its next ten years with more users and daily tweets than ever before, and it continues to make improvements.

Bird Beginnings   27

More and more young adults are using Twitter to keep up on the news, chat with others, share jokes, and make friends.

Twitter Takes Over

Over the last ten years or so, the world has witnessed (and participated in) the rise of Twitter. From one humble first tweet, it has quickly expanded. Today, people are tweeting all over the world, and at all hours. Companies, politicians, celebrities, and grandparents all have Twitter accounts. Some people have multiple accounts, allowing them to engage in several online communities at once. It has changed the way we read and digest news. It has become a place for commentary on everything happening in the world. So, what does this mean for us? What does constant social media access mean for our physical health, our mental health, our attention spans, and our emotions? How does it affect our day-to-day lives? And how can we lessen the damage it has caused?

Screen Time: How Much Is Too Much?

Twitter is meant to be enjoyed throughout the day. When a person first wakes up, he or she can open the app or website and see what is happening in other time zones. People check it for news in the middle of the day. Many fall asleep with phone in hand, dozing off to the glow of a screen and the scroll of Twitter updates. Some find it impossible to watch sports or television shows without checking Twitter for the wider commentary. When it comes to celebrity incidents or natural disasters? Twitter is the place to get up-to-the-moment updates and opinions.

All of this on-demand content is great. It keeps people informed. People are thinking and talking about issues, events, people, and places. However, research suggests that there should be limits and boundaries when it comes to screen time. This is especially true for children. Though the first studies on the subject have barely concluded, there are a few things we know for sure. First, children under eighteen account for one in three internet users worldwide. That means that one-third of all people on the internet are children and teens. The way they are accessing the internet is changing. While families used to invest in desktop computers or personal computers (PCs), today the internet is going mobile. More and more people, young and old, use phones and tablets to access the internet. This includes apps like Twitter.

All of this screen time has led researchers to focus money and time on studying the effects of screens, social

Some people worry that family time is being taken over by technology. Kids and adults can find it hard to disconnect from their screens.

media, and apps. But the results are split. Some experts believe that humans can form addictions to screens and applications, and that children are especially susceptible. On average, eight to eighteen year olds spend about seven hours on screens each day! This time includes multitasking, like having the television on in the background at dinner. Further research has shown that excessive screen time can lead to emotional problems, hyperactivity, social difficulties, and poor performance in school. Too much time on a phone, tablet, computer, or TV can also have negative effects on a person's sleep. These may seem like reasons to pull the plug on Twitter and other websites, especially for kids, but there are arguments for its use too. With screens, we are better connected than ever before. Youth have easy access to nearly unlimited amounts of information. Sites like Twitter can help people connect, form ideas, develop arguments, and learn about issues. As long as the time is reasonably limited, many professionals believe that social media and screens in general can be positive additions to our lives.

The Dark Side of Twitter

So, if a little social media time each day is OK, does that mean that Twitter is harmless? Not exactly. In addition to concerns about sleep, behavior, addiction, and attention spans, Twitter has always had its fair share of negativity that comes along with the platform. Twitterbots, trolls, and hackers can make the world of Twitter a scary and uncertain place.

Bots

When you first sign up for Twitter, you choose accounts to "follow" that will show up in the news feed, or homepage. You might choose friends, celebrities, or brands that you like. Based on this use, you might assume that all Twitter pages are run by real people. Unfortunately, there are tons of accounts that aren't people at all. They are Twitterbots, also known as "bots." A bot is an account controlled by software instead of a person. All on its own, this software can post tweets, retweet, follow, like, and even send direct messages. Sometimes, you may think you're interacting with another person, but you're actually tweeting with a bot!

Some bots behave badly, while others are used for good. An example of a "good" bot is one that automatically updates with the weather, information about natural disasters, funny memes, or even suggestions about how to practice self-care. Following one of these bots might feel like signing up for an email list or a helpful service.

Other bots are not helpful. They can spew inappropriate content and spread lies. During the 2016 US presidential election, bots that tweeted misinformation were an issue. Even some top politicians and journalists mistakenly retweeted content from bots. They were used to spread lies, spam, and show fake "support" for candidates. Those who have interest in a particular candidate, such as a business, organization, or even a foreign country, have used bots to influence US voters.

Trolls

While bots spread harmful information using automated software, internet trolls are real people who are determined to hurt others online. Trolls like to start fights, bully others, and disrupt discussions. Trolling is often considered a type of online harassment. If you thought that bullying was limited to school hallways or recess, it's not. Adult trolls are just like grown-up bullies who viciously attack others. At first, they may pretend to be a part of the legitimate discussion or group. Then, all of a sudden, a troll will post inaccurate information or intense, hateful words. To a troll, this behavior is funny and amusing. To others, it hurts. Because these trolls behave so badly, they hide behind fake usernames and accounts. It is often difficult to find the real identity behind a troll account on Twitter.

Twitter has written policies to try to stop the practice of trolling. When someone experiences trolling online, he or she can report the abuse to Twitter, but that does not mean the problem will be solved. Twitter's content is not monitored. People facing harassment and similar treatment can take action to stop this treatment, such as blocking users, but Twitter itself will not take action unless the user is in violation of Twitter's rules. Because Twitter has not released data on the amount of abuse that occurs on its site, some nonprofit organizations have taken it into their own hands. Multiple organizations, such as Amnesty International, have asked users to share their stories so that they can track the data and share it.

Hackers

Occasionally, the issues on Twitter grow far past bullying, trolling, or harassment. Hacking is a huge problem on the internet. Twitter has not been immune to the practice. No matter how secure a site may be, it can still be hacked by skilled criminals. A hacker is someone who uses technology to break into a computer network. Once he or she has access, the hacker can steal information like passwords, credit card numbers, and personal details. Sometimes

Hackers can be very intelligent, fast, and vicious. They can work as a team or alone. There are hackers all over the world.

hacking groups do this to steal information or just to show how powerful they are. Hacking is also a tool used by some countries to weaken the governments and businesses of other nations. Because hacking is a crime that you can't see, it can be a little creepy! Luckily, most sites and companies have security in place to deal with hackers. Usually, hacks can be stopped before they've been fully carried out.

At times, Twitter has battled hackers. Hackers have taken over specific Twitter accounts, like Jeep and Burger King. In these attacks, hackers might post false tweets (such as the "news" that Burger King had been purchased by McDonald's), change profile pictures to new photos, or steal the information of accounts' followers. The effects are usually temporary, but they can shake you! It never feels good to see your information stolen by another person, even if you're the owner of a large company. Other than keeping your password complicated, secure, and up-to-date, there isn't much that a Twitter user can do to combat hacking. It's up to Twitter to manage its own cybersecurity.

Privacy

When we think of security on the internet, some of the first things that come to mind might be hacking and harassment from bots/trolls. But one of the biggest buzzwords in today's world is "privacy." On social media sites, user information is often shared and sold to third parties. Third parties might be marketers, businesses, or even political organizations interested in knowing all about us. Legally, these social media sites have to publish privacy policies and user agreements, all of which are "agreed to" by users when they sign up. When you get a Twitter account, you just check a box after reading through the policy. Do most people read the entire document? Probably not.

Recently, Facebook has come under fire for its choice to share user information with marketers and others. When you log on to Facebook, you can see ads that are targeted toward things you probably like. Facebook knows you like these things because it knows what you browse on the rest of the internet. For many people, this feels nosy! So, people rush back to read the privacy policy and change their privacy settings on the site. Facebook has taken most of the heat for privacy issues, especially

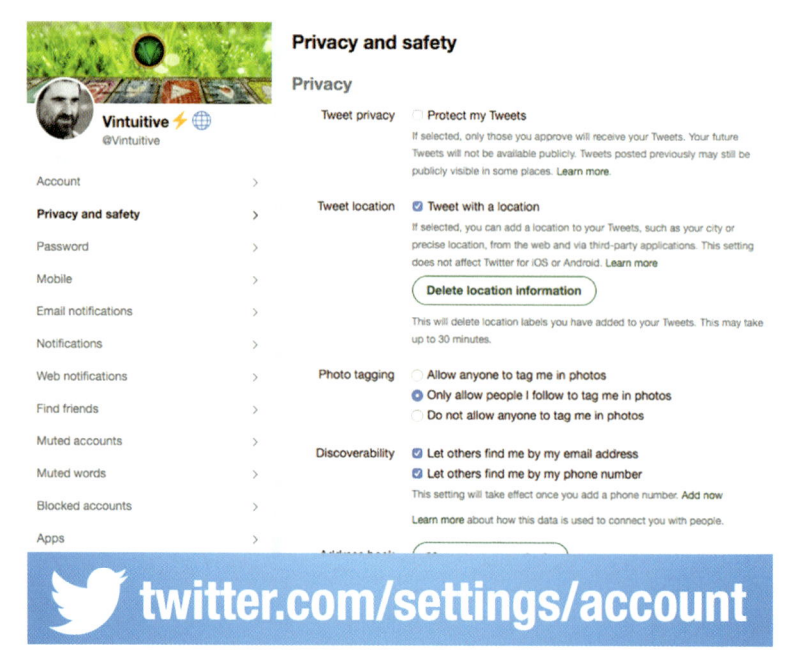

Privacy and safety are huge issues on social media. It is important to pay attention to your privacy settings whenever you post online.

following the 2016 presidential election in the United States. During that period, ads and content were used to target specific voters.

As a social media site, Twitter deals with similar privacy issues. In 2018, it was forced to update its policy to comply with new rules from the European Union. Just like Facebook, Twitter tracks the websites we visit, information from our devices, and personal information from people we contact online. It does this in order to make ads that are targeted. Companies often suggest that these ads are more relevant and provide a better experience to users. This may be somewhat true, but it remains an issue of privacy. Twitter, like Facebook, gives users the choice to opt out of much of the data usage. You can also keep Twitter from tracking your devices and tailoring ads to fit you. Ranked by sheer number of users, Facebook is dealing with much more data on a daily basis. But that doesn't mean Twitter doesn't need to secure its networks and keep its users' information safe.

Twitter Around the World

Sometimes, the world of social media might feel like a free-for-all. Twitter is used by the public, so it must be open to anything, right? No rules? Well, not exactly. Twitter has many pages of rules and policies. This is especially true when it comes to violent or illegal content. In the United States, as well as in other countries, tweets can be blocked, or "withheld," if they violate the law. These tweets may be visible outside the borders of that country, but they cannot be accessed while inside. For example, recently, the German and French governments requested that certain tweets be withheld. The European Union, of which France and Germany are a part, has a code of conduct that guards against hate speech. That includes hateful tweets. This means that users in those countries will not be able to see withheld tweets, but users in other countries may. Twitter reports each year on the number of withheld tweets and accounts. However, it does not list the actual accounts or tweets themselves.

In some countries, including North Korea, China, and Iran, Twitter is blocked completely. China blocked the site in 2009, but experts suggest that there are still millions of users within the country. Essentially, users find ways to access internet networks that exist outside the country, and then they log in to Twitter through those networks. The Chinese government can only censor internet content accessed within its borders. Other popular websites, including Facebook, Blogger, and even Google, are completely blocked inside mainland China.

In Iran, there has been a country-wide ban of Twitter since 2009. At that time, an Iranian presidential election was being held, and the government feared that protests could be organized on Twitter. It's true that many protests, demonstrations, and rallies have been organized on the site. In general, Iran has blocked many popular websites, including Facebook, YouTube, and even shopping and sports sites.

North Korea may be the country that most would expect to have blocked Twitter from the start. Its

WHO'S THAT BIRD?

One of the most memorable parts of Twitter is its logo. Since its beginning, Twitter has had a blue bird logo. The first was designed by Simon Oxley in 2006. He put it up for sale on his graphic design website, where the Twitter team bought it for only $15. The original logo featured two tiny feet. It was skinny and realistic—like a real bird! In 2009, Biz Stone and Philip Pascuzzo worked together to create a more cartoonish bird with flying wings and an open beak. Since then, the logo has been tweaked every couple of years.

Many wonder about the logo's name. Since 2006, the founders have said that the bird's name is Larry the Bird. He is named after Larry Bird, a basketball legend from the Boston Celtics.

The Twitter logo and the company's signature blue color have become iconic and easily recognizable.

Twitter Takes Over 39

government is a dictatorship. It is highly restrictive of information flowing within the country. Viewers can choose from three television stations—all country-owned and operated. Internet is also highly restricted and is usually only accessed by foreigners and members of the government. Schoolchildren do not research their papers online. When people have questions, they don't hop on Google to find the answer. However, it wasn't until April 2016 that the country began to block Twitter, Facebook, and other social media sites. The government reported that they were concerned with the online spread of information and needed to take action. Before 2016, the North Korean government operated its own Twitter, YouTube, and other accounts. These accounts, written entirely in Korean, were used to push the government's ideas and agenda.

China, North Korea, and Iran aren't the only countries that choose to withhold tweets. During a time of protest in 2014, Venezuela temporarily blocked pictures on Twitter. Turkey, Russia, Pakistan, Egypt, and other countries have participated in withholding on the site, often in response to protests. It is Twitter's policy to work with individual countries to decide what is and is not accessible within each country's borders.

Embracing Twitter Internationally

While some countries choose to block some or all of Twitter, other nations have embraced it. Many world leaders have turned to Twitter as a way to connect with their citizens. It can even be a way to practice diplomacy. President Barack Obama, Queen Elizabeth II,

Even world leaders, like German chancellor Angela Merkel, use their phones for business, communication, and to see what's going on across the globe.

Pope Francis, Jordan's Queen Rania, and the leaders of countless other countries, including the United States, are all active Twitter users. People like and retweet their tweets. The things they say can have an effect on the entire world. President Donald Trump, in particular, has been extremely talkative on Twitter throughout his presidency. Sometimes, the things Trump tweets are a surprise to others in his administration!

Each world leader treats Twitter differently. Trump uses it to share his personal beliefs and try to gain support from followers. Other leaders have used the platform to inspire, to share important information, or to be silly and down-to-earth with the public. Many of them have millions of followers.

In 2017, Twitter started to receive feedback from users that they wanted to see some content from world leaders blocked. Their tweets could be read as inappropriate, hateful, or even violent. Twitter shared an official response:

> *Twitter is here to serve and help advance the global, public conversation. Elected world leaders play a critical role in that conversation because of their outsized impact on our society.*
>
> *Blocking a world leader from Twitter or removing their controversial Tweets would hide important information people should be able to see and debate. It would also not silence that leader, but it would certainly hamper necessary discussion around their words and actions.*

This language is just an example of how dedicated the Twitter team is to ensuring that their platform is as open and accessible as possible. They would like it to inspire discussion, debate, and critique, even if some of those conversations are hard.

Outages

As we can see, Twitter is a very important social network to many people. Some rely on it for news, some check it for updates after disasters, and others use it to socialize or to

DID YOU KNOW:

Twitter isn't just for friends and family. Many businesses, large and small, have Twitter accounts. They use these to advertise, answer questions, and respond to complaints from customers. Over 80 percent of the top businesses in the world use Twitter.

Before Twitter could handle all of its users, it would sometimes post the "fail whale," an image that represented website traffic being too "heavy."

teach. When Twitter isn't available, an outage can cause a huge uproar. People go to other social media channels to vent about the platform, angry and frustrated. But when an outage happens, there isn't anything a regular user can do. Outages usually occur due to complex technical problems. Online, one can find "outage maps" where outages are reported and logged in a visual map. These might be broken down into categories like "mobile app down," "website down," and "everything down," so that users know what exactly is happening.

In its first few years, Twitter had frequent outages. The company even designed a "fail whale." This was a drawing of a whale being lifted out of the ocean by tiny orange birds. This drawing would appear on the website when it was down or had too many users online. Today, outages still occur, but they are less frequent. They mostly surround popular events or notable incidents. Those are the times when Twitter is likely to get overloaded.

Twitter Takes Over 43

Hashtags are often used in protests, rallies, and political events. These hashtags refer to an important movement concerning sexual harassment that occurred in 2017.

CHAPTER FOUR

Leaving a Legacy

There are always new websites and apps being created and introduced to society. Social media sites come and go, as do news sites, games, and social networks. However, Twitter seems to be here to stay. Throughout the years, the number of users has increased tremendously. Not only that, but its other features have become extremely popular. The direct messaging service through Twitter is a popular way to meet people, make friends, and even date. It seems like each year, Twitter is releasing new updates that make the platform better. They have to do this in order to keep people interested, keep their brand relevant, and make sure that Twitter is still the main place for news and content online.

Features and Updates

Twitter began as a simple concept—quick status updates posted semi-publicly. The messages were short, just 140 characters, because the limit for SMS messages (texts) was just 160 characters. What began as a limitation turned into one of Twitter's signatures. The limit forced people to think big thoughts in fewer words. Users had to consider their words carefully before posting. In 2017, Twitter announced that it would double its character limit, increasing it to 280 characters. Users weren't exactly delighted. Some thought it was a good idea, but others worried about longer tweets clogging up the feed. However, CEO Jack Dorsey noted that during testing of the new limits, people still wrote within the old limit most of the time. Even though they were given the option to write longer posts, dedicated Twitter users stuck to what they knew best—short, succinct tweets. Today, the 280-character limit is still in place.

In addition to messages, Twitter has evolved to include all sorts of content. It now has polls, videos, and pictures. Streaming video was added in 2015 with the purchase of Periscope, a streaming app. Now, videos are integrated into the feed, and Twitter hopes to introduce twenty-four/seven streaming video in the future. This type of feature can already be seen in "Facebook live" posts on the competitor's website and app. The longer they wait, the further behind in the streaming game Twitter will be, but the company is working to catch up. In 2015, polls went live on Twitter. This gave users the ability to give quick surveys to their

Periscope is a video-streaming app that was purchased by Twitter in 2015.

users. Since then, Instagram has adopted the popular feature for itself, and in 2017, Facebook introduced its own polls for its news feed. It seems that great ideas get passed around the social media circle quickly.

Before videos and polls, Twitter had pictures. But you couldn't always upload a photo directly onto the platform. For many years, that task was handled by third-party sites and apps. Twitpic is one example. Using Twitpic, people could upload their photos and have them inserted into tweets. It was a slow process, but it worked. You couldn't add pictures any other way. Eventually, the company figured out how to integrate photos into its tweets directly, and Twitpic and other businesses closed down. At the same time, Twitter decided that photos from Instagram wouldn't be allowed to appear through Twitter. Instagram

Leaving a Legacy 47

There seem to be new social media apps every day. Each has its own unique purpose, audience, and branding. These are just a few examples of the numerous options available online.

is a popular photo-sharing app, and many people like to share their Instagram stories on other platforms.

The Twitter Experience

Because so many people use Twitter with such dedication, you know that users' experiences must be important. Twitter isn't just another way to update your friends. For many, it has been a way to connect, build community, and form a valuable social network. Activism is sparked on Twitter. You can follow events as they happen. Every day, millions of people engage in conversation around the events, people, places, and issues that matter most to them.

One of the most powerful examples of how Twitter has been used to spark and maintain social movements is #BlackLivesMatter, or #BLM. The hashtag first emerged in 2013. That summer, there were high rates of young black males being shot and killed. Some of the cases were controversial. They appeared in the news every day. As the summer dragged on and other cases of violence against black men and boys occurred, the phrase popped up over and over again. By August, it was being used tens of thousands of times each day. From activists and organizers to entertainers, news organizations, young people, and even those who were opposed to the movement, the hashtag was in heavy use on Twitter. It spread to other social media sites, too, such as YouTube, Facebook, and Instagram. With the help of Twitter, Black Lives Matter was able to solidify itself as a strong, standalone movement that hasn't slowed down or disappeared. In fact, it continues to gain momentum.

Following the eruption of #BlackLivesMatter, a community developed on Twitter that is now commonly known as "black Twitter." Essentially, this consists of

A well-known hashtag can send a loud message. #Resist has been used to show resistance against US president Donald Trump and his various policies.

Leaving a Legacy 49

black Twitter users from around the world who are thinking and talking about black identity in the United States—on Twitter. The community has engaged with multiple hashtags and worked tirelessly to bring about conversation and change within the country. The hashtags #BlackOnCampus, #BlackLivesMatter, #SayHerName, and #HandsUpDontShoot are all components of black Twitter. While the community is built around people of color leading the discussions, the public nature of Twitter gives the entire world a window into the experiences, opinions, stories, and statements being shared. It has served to both widen and deepen the conversation on race within the United States.

Other causes have used hashtags to unite communities in conversation. Some were even more deliberate than #BLM. The #GivingTuesday conversation was created by the UN Foundation. The foundation hoped to capitalize on Black Friday excitement. On the Tuesday after Thanksgiving, people are encouraged to give to their favorite nonprofit organizations, especially after they see the hashtag on Twitter. Between 2012 and 2016, the hashtag was used over three million times and generated tens of millions of dollars in donations to various nonprofits. In fact, hashtags have proven to be a driving force when it comes to fundraising. Phrases like #PrayforJapan and #PrayforParis have directed funds to countries and cities affected by natural disasters and terrorist attacks. These hashtags not only show emotional support to victims, but they direct funds toward people most in need.

COMPLAINTS AND COMPLIMENTS

Twitter has revolutionized the ways in which businesses engage with their customers. Instead of being forced to call a customer service line, customers can talk to the company's Twitter account. There, their issue will be dealt with immediately. No company wants negative reviews sitting in its Twitter profile. This has forced companies to work hard to respond to users' requests, even though the method is often easier than traditional phone banks of customer service representatives. Instead, a few trained professionals can read and reply to tweets all day long. These replies and likes help people feel heard and appreciated by the companies that engage with them on Twitter.

Additionally, Twitter helps companies conduct undercover market research. A shoe brand might log on to see which pairs are being discussed the most on Twitter. They also may see which items aren't popular, and they will hear those complaints loud and clear, rather than simply waiting (a long time) for the product to be purchased in a store. Using Twitter, brands can create their own personalities and relationships with customers.

Over the years, Twitter has taken the opportunity to upgrade some of its hashtags in response to major events. In 2015, the United States Supreme Court ruled in favor of same-sex marriage. Twitter greeted the news by including an automatic heart emoji each time someone tweeted #LoveWins. The hashtag was used nearly thirteen million times—even President Obama used the popular hashtag when he heard the news of the court's ruling. The emoji also inspired other networks to add rainbow-colored features to their sites during the week of the ruling.

DID YOU KNOW:
Many churches are embracing Twitter. Some encourage attendees to tweet during the service. Other churches have their own Twitter pages. Even the Catholic Church—and many of its leaders—has a Twitter account!

When a person is searching for a subject to follow on Twitter, like #LoveWins or #BLM, he or she can go to the list of "Trending Topics" and see what others are talking about online. Many days, this looks less like a list of nonprofits and more like a list of prime-time television. More and more, Twitter has become a destination for TV watchers. During shows like *The Bachelor* and the Super Bowl, Twitter usage skyrockets. Not only do people want to joke about events and share their opinions, but they want to read what others have to say about their favorite programs. From this trend, a new phrase has

Many people use Twitter while they watch television. This can be a great way to interact with people around the world while sharing a common experience.

emerged: the "second screen." The second screen refers to the practice of reading Twitter or posting on Twitter while watching a television show. This is a particularly popular activity during live events such as the Super Bowl or awards shows.

Today, when you're watching television, you might see a hashtag pop up in the lower corner of your screen. That's the hashtag that the TV network would like you to use to discuss the episode on Twitter. The relationship also works in reverse—all four major TV networks have a deal with Twitter to include video clips of their programming within the Twitter feed itself. Today, that second screen has become almost a necessity. If you aren't tweeting about a show, are you really watching it? The same could be said of sports events, which are very popular on Twitter. The site is one of the first places to go to get real-time updates on professional sports teams, as well as college sports.

Leaving a Legacy   53

What's Next?

Now that Twitter has captured many people's leisure time, activism, churches, sports events, and more, where does it go from here? While Twitter still has fewer users than Facebook, it continues to attract new people and encourage more tweeting. It adds millions of users each year and has recently begun to make a small profit. Advertisements help. Twitter makes money from advertisers who put ads on the site. The company hopes to make even more

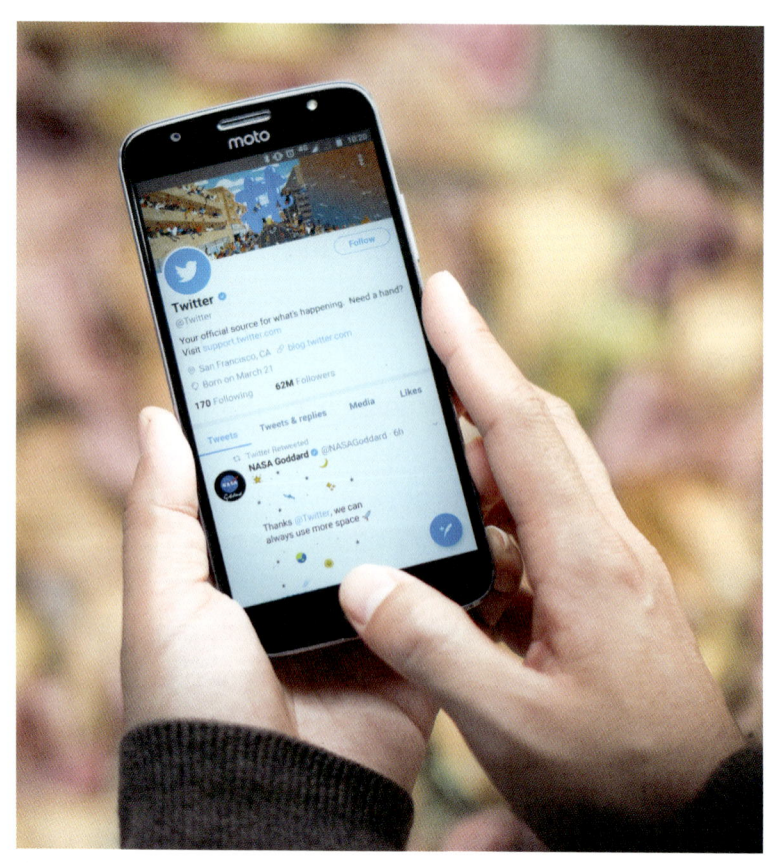

Twitter is very user-friendly. Its "feeds" are easy to navigate and update quickly with just the touch of a finger.

money from advertisers with its twenty-four-hour live video stream. If people are watching video on Twitter, they will see more ads. Then, Twitter will make more money. Twitter will be streaming content for ESPN, Disney, MLB, NBC, and many other channels. Aside from video, it continues to gain followers for its main service—tweeting short, to-the-point messages. Celebrities, politicians, and other entertainers are constantly being called out for the things they write on Twitter. The platform has created drama, intrigue, and a lot of apologies from those who said the wrong thing. On Twitter, anything can happen. People fight, fall in love, find careers, become addicted to their screens, and make lifelong friends.

One of the best things about Twitter is how open it is. Not only can Twitter users interact with others, but they can talk to almost anyone in the world, as long as that person has Twitter. With mobile technology, people are now able to tweet from almost anywhere using phones and tablets, rather than PCs alone. For those who are still dedicated to the internet browser version, that remains as well.

It's hard to say what will come next for Twitter. It probably won't change its role as a social media tool. But over the years, it has introduced features that have made the product more user-friendly and fun. As long as people continue to see the benefits of logging on and joining in the Twitter conversation, they will create accounts, and the dialogue will grow. At the moment, it looks like the company is still in the midst of a decades-long growth spurt that isn't about to slow down.

GLOSSARY

application A computer program that performs assigned tasks.

blog A regular series of relatively short, personal posts on a website.

bot A type of software that controls a Twitter account.

censor To suppress words, ideas, art, writings, films, and more because they are thought to be offensive or obscene.

client A piece of software that accesses the service being offered by Twitter.

hacker A person who tries to weaken or destroy a computer network.

IPO An initial public offering, or the moment when a company sells shares of itself to the public.

outage When Twitter isn't working and needs to shut down for a while.

PC A personal computer that stays in one place, rather than being easily moved.

platform The software or hardware that provides a base for another technology.

second screen The practice of using a mobile device while watching television.

share A piece of ownership in a company, often referring to and used interchangeably with "stock."

social media Websites, apps, blogs, and other things that allow users to create and share content with other people.

stock market A place where parts, or stocks, of certain companies can be bought and sold.

troll A person who hopes to disrupt or destroy online conversations by posting alarming content.

verified account An account that is of interest to the public, and which usually has a large number of followers.

withhold To block a tweet or account from access inside a particular country.

FURTHER INFORMATION

Books

Cuban, Mark, Shaan Patel, and Ian McCue. *Kid Start-Up: How YOU Can Be an Entrepreneur.* New York: Diversion Books, 2018.

McKee, Jonathan. *The Teen's Guide to Social Media and Mobile Devices: 21 Tips to Wise Posting in an Insecure World.* Uhrichsville, OH: Shiloh Run Press, 2017.

Ramberg, JJ, and Melanie Staggs. *The Startup Club.* Herndon, Virginia: Mascot Books, 2017.

Raum, Elizabeth. *Social Media Savvy: Facts and Figures About Selfies, Smartphones, and Standing Out.* Mankato, MN: Capstone Press, 2018.

Rowell, Rebecca. *Social Media: Like It or Leave It.* Mankato, MN: Compass Point Books, 2015.

Websites

Blogger

http://www.blogger.com

On this site, you can create and publish your own blog—for free!

Bystander Revolution

http://www.bystanderrevolution.org

Take a stand against bullying. Visit this site to learn more about how you can stop cyberbullying and other forms of harassment.

NaNoWriMo

https://ywp.nanowrimo.org

Love to write and share stories online? Try National Novel Writers Month, a month dedicated to writing fiction.

Youth Radio

https://youthradio.org

If you're interested in what other kids and teens have to say about the issues of today, read and listen to their voices on Youth Radio! There are articles, blogs, interviews, and more.

Videos

Full Interview: Jack Dorsey

https://www.youtube.com/watch?v=Nx46su211io

This 2017 interview with Twitter cofounder Jack Dorsey features Andrew Ross Sorkin of the *New York Times*.

The Illustrated History of Twitter

https://www.youtube.com/watch?v=NzRkszaGBbY

This fun video shares the history of Twitter in a fast-paced visual format.

What Is Twitter?

https://www.commonsensemedia.org/videos/what-is-twitter

If you need a quick, one-minute description of Twitter, watch this video! It clearly explains the platform.

SELECTED BIBLIOGRAPHY

Becket, Adam. "The 10 Most Liked Tweets of All Time Are Dominated by Obama." *Business Insider*. August 16, 2017. http://www.businessinsider.com/10-most-liked-tweets-of-all-time-2017-8.

Douglas, Nick. "Twitter Blows Up at SXSW Conference." *Gawker*. March 12, 2007. http://gawker.com/243634/twitter-blows-up-at-sxsw-conference.

Johnson, Mark. "The History of Twitter." Socialnomics. January 23, 2013. https://socialnomics.net/2013/01/23/the-history-of-twitter.

Kollewe, Julia. "Twitter Makes First Quarterly Profit In Its History." *Guardian*. February 8, 2018. https://www.theguardian.com/technology/2018/feb/08/twitter-makes-first-quarterly-profit-history.

Lee, Dave. "How Twitter Changed the World, Hashtag-by-Hashtag." BBC. November 7, 2013. http://www.bbc.com/news/technology-24802766.

McIntosh, Neil. "Google Buys Blogger Web Service." *Guardian*. February 18, 2003. https://www.theguardian.com/business/2003/feb/18/digitalmedia.citynews.

Neal, Ryan W. "Who Is Noah Glass? 9 Things To Know About The Ousted Twitter Founder." *International Business Times*. October 10, 2013. http://www.ibtimes.com/who-noah-glass-9-things-know-about-ousted-twitter-founder-1421134.

Pandell, Lexi. "An Oral History of the #Hashtag." *Wired*. May 19, 2017. https://www.wired.com/2017/05/oral-history-hashtag.

Pepitone, Julianne. "Twitter's Hacking Problem." CNN. February 21, 2013. http://money.cnn.com/2013/02/21/technology/social/twitter-hacking/index.html.

Spangler, Todd. "Twitter CEO Jack Dorsey Declines Compensation for Third Straight Year." *Variety*. April 11, 2018. http://variety.com/2018/digital/news/twitter-jack-dorsey-declines-compensation-2017-1202750870.

Statt, Nick. "To Twitter CEO and Back Again: A Timeline of Jack Dorsey's Rise." *Verge*. October 5, 2015. https://www.theverge.com/2015/10/5/9457277/jack-dorsey-twitter-ceo-timeline.

Stone, Madeline. "The Fabulous Life of Jack Dorsey, Twitter's Billionaire CEO." *Business Insider*. October 5, 2015. http://www.businessinsider.com/fabulous-life-of-twitter-ceo-jack-dorsey-2015-6.

Vanian, Jonathan. "Twitter CEO Jack Dorsey Wants the Public's Help in Measuring Twitter's 'Health.'" *Fortune*. March 1, 2018. http://fortune.com/2018/03/01/twitter-jack-dorsey-health-abuse.

Wynter, Amanda. "Bringing Twitter to the Classroom." *Atlantic*. September 15, 2014. https://www.theatlantic.com/education/archive/2014/09/the-case-for-having-class-discussions-on-twitter/379777.

INDEX

Page numbers in **boldface** are illustrations.

accessibility, 9, 22, 29–31, 38, 40, 42
active users, 7, 21, 25, 41
addiction, 16, 31–32, 55
advertisement, 26, 42, 54–55
application, 5–7, 9, 10, 21, 23, 25–26, 30–31, 43, 45–48
attention span, 29, 32

#BlackLivesMatter, **11**, 48–50, 52
blog, 19, 21–23
Blogger, 21–23, 38
bot, 9, 32–33, 35
bullying, 6, 11, 33–34
businesses, 17, 19, 21–23, 33, 35, 42, 47, 51

censor, 38
chief executive officer (CEO), 16, **19**, 20, 46
client, 9

community, 29, 48–50
customer service, 51

diplomacy, 40
direct messaging, 32, 45
disasters, 10, 30, 32, 42, 50
Dorsey, Jack, 14, 16, 18–21, **19**, 23, 46

Facebook, 5–7, 17–18, 21, 25, 27, 36–38, 40, 46–47, 49, 54
fail whale, 43, **43**

Glass, Noah, 14–16, 23–24

hacker, 32, 34–35, **34**
hashtag, 24–26, 48–50, 52–53
hate, 33, 38, 41

IPO, 26–27

LGBTQ, 11
LiveJournal, 19

62   How Twitter Changed the World

logo, 39, **39**

Messina, Chris, 25–26

news, 5–8, 10–11, 14–15, 18, 29–30, 32, 35, 42, 45, 47, 49, 52

Obama, Barack, 7, **8**, 40, 52
Odeo, 13–16, 21–23, 27
outage, 42–43
Oxley, Simon, 39

PC, 30, 55
platform, 6, 9, 10–11, 13, 19, 21–22, 24–25, 27, 32, 41–43, 45, 47–48, 55
podcast, 13–14
privacy, 35–37
protests, 38, 40, **44**

rules, 34, 37

screen time, 30–31

second screen, 53, **53**
security, 35
share, 5–6, 10–11, 13–15, 20, 21, 26–27, 32, 34–36, 41, 48, 50, 52
Silicon Valley, 18, 22–23
social media, 5–6, 10–11, 13, 21–22, 24, 29–32, 35, 37, 40, 43, 45, 47, 49, 55
stock market, 26–27
Stone, Biz, **12**, 14, 16, 22–23, 25, 39
SXSW, **12**, 17, 24–25

troll, 32–35
Trump, Donald, 41

verified account, 10
video streaming, 23, 46–47, 53, 55

Williams, Evan, 14–16, 19, 21–23
withhold, 37–38, 40

Index 63

ABOUT THE AUTHOR

Kaitlyn Duling believes in the power of words to change hearts, minds, and, ultimately, actions. An avid reader and writer who grew up in Illinois, she now resides in Washington, DC. She knows that knowledge of the past is the key to our future, and wants to make sure that all children and families have access to high-quality information. She is an avid social media user who has been tweeting since 2009.